Thank you to my amazing, supportive

All rights reserved.
No part of this book may be reproduced or transmitted by any means, except as permitted by UK copyright law or the author.

All rights reserved.
For permission to publish, distribute or otherwise reproduce this work, please contact the author at Andrea6uk@yahoo.co.uk.

Copyright 2024 © by Andrea Connor

Can you spot this little guy on every page?

"Ouch! I've just been hit on my head."
He looked around and then he said.
"What on earth happened, what just hit me?"
In the corner of his eye he saw a bird flee.

He was feeling confused, lost and dazed.
On top of all that his poor eyes were glazed.
Looking down his shell was smashed on the ground.
Also, what is that horrible sound?

His ears were ringing and his head was sore.
His beautiful home was a mess on the floor.
The poor little guy was confused, withered and pale.
His eyes were spinning, what a pitiful snail.

Without my shell I'm exposed to snow, rain and hail!
Now I've lost my house, where will they deliver my mail?
He had to think fast, he would need a new home.
He was still feeling dizzy so he let out a moan.

He would search high and low for a new abode.
No time like the present he glides down the road.
He slithered and slugged through water then mud.
He hoped to find a house that wasn't too crud.
On top of a rock he spied an ice cream cone.
Could this be the answer to his new home?

With the cone on his back he crawled along.
When the rain came down he knew something was wrong.
The cone was now wet and began to dissolve.
Just another problem for him to solve.
He chittered and chattered which made him feel sad.
He decided to keep going so he didn't feel bad.

Moving on quickly he felt much brighter.
Without the soggy cone he felt a lot lighter.
He started to smile for he knew he was smart.
So now back to work on mending his shell and his heart.

He came by some litter, an old crisp packet.
It kept the rain off just like a jacket.
It felt nice and warm and protected his back.
But it crinkled and crackled and felt a bit slack.

The packet was noisy it was hard to think.
Then he got a whiff of a strong cheesy stink.
Off with the packet and wash the stench away.
All his high hopes were starting to fray.

What's that noise? He heard a giggle and a caw.
When he looked around there stood a jackdaw.
The snail finally asked, "Why are you laughing at me?"
The Jackdaw smirked, "Ah you will soon see!"
She then flew away with a smirk on her face.
The snail thought, my word! How mean! What a disgrace!

He wasn't having much luck looking on the ground.
He would get a better look on top of that mound.
When he got higher he could see such a long way.
He noticed lots of strawberries, now time to play.
As he moved on his memory came back.
He remembered the bird and why she attacked.

The jackdaw was getting revenge for me scoffing her food.
I couldn't help it, the strawberries tasted so good.
He noticed his friends all huddled together.
Discussing and planning what they'll eat for dinner.

When the snail realised he started to giggle.
It moved down his belly and made it all jiggle.
I'm a slug not a snail! And that shell wasn't my home!
I can now move around and it's easier to roam.
The slug was so happy that he wasn't a snail.
He was a slug with friends and a wonderful tale.

The End...
Of the slug's story......

The Jackdaw

Who's been eating my strawberries again?
Last time I counted there was a total of ten.
Now all of my strawberries are mostly gone.
At this rate there will be nothing left on this lawn.
It's that slug and his friends who keep coming back.
I need to think of a way to launch an attack.

How dare he, those strawberries are mine.
I think it's now time I put up a sign.
I need to find something to drop on his head.
Now with that thought, off the little bird sped.

She spotted a shell while flying around.
She swooped down and lifted it up from the ground.
Now for revenge and to make that slug stop.
And on his head I will let the shell plop.

It will give him a warning and also a fright.
If he steals them again, he's not very bright.
The jackdaw flew over and dropped the shell.
It hit the slug on the head and he let out a yell.
The slug yelped, "Ouch! I've just been hit on my head."
The jackdaw was laughing inside as she fled.

She watched from afar as the slug looked confused.
The top of his head looked battered and bruised.
She followed the slug and watched what he did.
The slug found a cone and the jackdaw hid.

The jackdaw sniggered as the cone got wet.
He thinks he's a snail, how could he forget.
The slug was now wearing an old crisp packet.
The jackdaw giggled as it made such a racket.
It crinkled and crackled and looked really bad.
The jackdaw smiled, this is the most fun I've had.

The slug now moving faster, he'd picked up his pace.
He's heading for my strawberries to stuff his greedy face.
The slug reached his friends and they all had a giggle.
The jackdaw was so mad that her tail started to wiggle.
He's foiled my plan and I'm back to square one.
That slug is annoying and ruining my fun.

The jackdaw swooped down ready to protect her food.
Surely the slugs will stay away or are they just being rude.
But the slugs had decided on lettuce for dinner that day.
This made the jackdaw happy so she allowed them stay.

The End

Printed in Great Britain
by Amazon